BIG BEASTS
Tiger

Stephanie Turnbull

Published by Smart Apple Media
P.O. Box 1329
Mankato, MN 56002

Printed in the United States of America,
at Corporate Graphics in North Mankato, Minnesota.

Designed by Helen James
Edited by Mary-Jane Wilkins

Library of Congress Cataloging-in-Publication Data

Turnbull, Stephanie.
 Tiger / Steph Turnbull.
    p. cm. -- (Big beasts)
 Includes index.
 Summary: "An introduction on tigers, the big beasts in Asia.
Describes how tigers move, find food, communicate, and care for
their young. Also mentions the different kinds of tigers and their
differences"--Provided by publisher.
 ISBN 978-1-59920-837-4 (hardcover, library bound)
 1. Tiger--Juvenile literature. I. Title.
 QL737.C23T796 2013
 599.756--dc23

                        2012004116

Photo acknowledgements
page 1 iStockphoto/Thinkstock; 3 iStockphoto/Thinkstock;
4l Tom Brakefield/Thinkstock; 4r tratong/Shutterstock;
5 Scott E Read/Shutterstock; 6 iStockphoto/Thinkstock;
7 iStockphoto/Thinkstock; 8 Laurin Rinder/Shutterstock;
9 Ryan McVay/Thinkstock; 11 TRyburn/Shutterstock;
12 Jupiterimages/Thinkstock; 14 beltsazar/Shutterstock;
15 Jupiterimages/Thinkstock; 16 Steve Wilson/Shutterstock;
17 Marko5/Shutterstock; 18 Tom Brakefield/Thinkstock;
19 iStockphoto/Thinkstock; 20 Hemera/Thinkstock;
21l Timothy Craig Lubcke/Shutterstock; 21r Jjustas/
Shutterstock; 23 Matthew Cole/Shutterstock
Cover Eric Isselée/Shutterstock

DAD0503b
072013
9 8 7 6 5 4 3 2

Contents

Tigers
are

huge!

Giant Cats

Tigers are the biggest wild cats in the world.
They live in Asia.

Bengal tigers
live in hot,
grassy lands.

A few Bengal tigers have white fur.

Siberian tigers
live in cold forests.
Their thick fur
keeps them warm.

Stay Away!

What tigers like best is lots of

S P A C E

to roam in...
alone.

They fight any other tigers who come near.

They love to cool off in water.

On the Prowl

As the sun sets, tigers pad silently along, searching for dinner.

Tigers have amazing eyesight.
They can see well in the dark.

Their ears perk up
to catch every sound.

Sneaky Hunting

When tigers spot a deer or antelope, they crouch low in the grass.

Their **stripes** help them hide.

Slowly they creep forward... closer and closer... then...

SPRING!

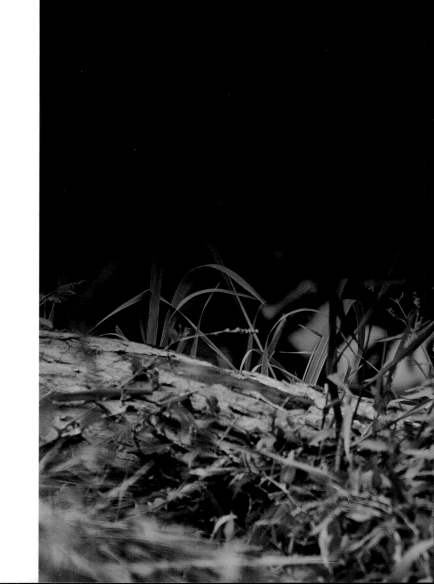

Attack!

Tigers pounce on their prey and drag it to the ground in a flash.

They kill the animal with one big bite.

They can eat the WHOLE animal in one meal.

Killer Claws

Tigers have long, razor-sharp claws that POP out when they attack.

They have five claws on each front paw, and four on each back paw.

Tigers scratch tree trunks to keep their claws clean and sharp.

Open Wide!

Tigers
have 30
terrifying
teeth.

The four long front teeth are for biting.
Each one is longer than your finger.

The other front teeth are for tearing meat.

Wide back teeth can slice chunks of flesh.

Big Babies

Tiger babies are called cubs.

At first they snuggle in a cozy den, drinking their mother's milk.

Bigger cubs like having play fights. They learn to hunt and look after themselves.

Tiger Talk

Tigers purr to say, "I'm happy," or, "I like you."

Angry growls mean, "Go away or I'll attack!"

GROWL

A loud roar means, "Here I am! Don't come near!"

RRAAARR!

21

BIG Facts

Tigers can be as long as you and two friends lying end to end.

The biggest tigers weigh the same as 100 pet cats.

Tigers can attack animals as big as crocodiles, bears and young elephants.

A big tiger
paw is the size
of this page.

Useful Words

den
A tiger's sleeping place. Tigers make dens in caves, hollow trees and thick grass.

pounce
To jump or spring on to something suddenly to catch it.

prey
An animal that is hunted by another animal.

Web Link
Go to this website for useful tiger facts and print-outs:
www.enchantedlearning.com/subjects/mammals/tiger